◆◆ PUEBLO STORYTELLER ◆◆

Text copyright © 1991 by Diane Hoyt-Goldsmith.
Photographs copyright © 1991 by Lawrence Migdale.
Text illustrations copyright © 1991 by Leonard Trujillo.
All rights reserved. Published by Scholastic Inc.,
730 Broadway, New York, NY 10003, by arrangement with
Holiday House, Inc.
Printed in the U.S.A.
ISBN 0-590-46264-4

       6 7 8 9 10   08   99 98 97 96 95

ACKNOWLEDGMENTS

In creating this book, we enjoyed the enthusiasm and cooperation of many
people. We would like to express our special appreciation to Mary, Leonard,
and April Trujillo for sharing their harmonious way of life with us. We greatly
enjoyed their friendship and generous hospitality during our visits to the
Cochiti Pueblo in New Mexico.

In addition, we would like to thank Glynn, Lisa, and Dawn Trujillo, Geri
Trujillo, and Justin Pecos for their help and participation.

We are grateful to Gabriel "Yellowbird" Trujillo of Cochiti Pueblo for sharing
his knowledge of drum making with us. Andy Garcia, of San Juan Pueblo, was
generous with his time and knowledge of pueblo dance traditions. We were
fortunate to see several performances of the dance group that he founded and
directs. We are thankful to him and his grandsons, Elmer and Curt, for showing
us the Buffalo Dance.

In addition, we were fortunate to have the good advice and assistance of
Pat Reck and Joyce Merrill at the Pueblo Indian Cultural Center in Albuquerque;
Marsha Bols, at the Museum of International Folk Art in Santa Fe; and the staff
at Eight Northern Indian Pueblos Council at San Juan.

The text illustrations included in this book are inspired by the decorations
on pottery made by Mary Trujillo's mother, Leonidas Tapia, of San Juan Pueblo,
and we include them to honor her memory.

For more information about the Storytellers, write to:
    Mary and Leonard Trujillo
    P.O. Box 147
    Cochiti Pueblo, New Mexico 87041

For more information about the Cochiti drums, write to:
    Gabriel "Yellowbird" Trujillo
    P.O. Box 72
    Cochiti Pueblo, New Mexico 87041

For more information about the pueblo dance group, write to:
    Andy Garcia
    P.O. Box 1055
    San Juan Pueblo, New Mexico 87566

PUEBLO STORYTELLER

BY DIANE HOYT-GOLDSMITH

PHOTOGRAPHS BY LAWRENCE MIGDALE

SCHOLASTIC INC.

New York Toronto London Auckland Sydney

This book is dedicated to
the loving memory
of April's mother,

Jo Ann Trujillo,

of Cochiti Pueblo, New Mexico

1956–1983

My name is April. I live with my grandparents in the Cochiti *(KOH-chi-tee)* Pueblo near Santa Fe, New Mexico. Pueblo *(PWEB-loh)* is a Spanish word that means "village" or "town." Our pueblo is very old. The Cochiti people have lived on these lands for many hundreds of years.

When I was a baby, my parents gave a special party to introduce me to their family and friends. On this occasion, I was given my Indian name, KU-tsi-ya-t'si *(KOO-tsee-yahtz)* which means "Lady Antelope" in Keres *(CARE-ees)*, the language of my people.

April wears a handmade pueblo blouse and manta (MON-tah). *The manta is a dress that covers one shoulder and is pinned on the side. Her jewelry was made by hand from silver and turquoise stones.*

Like many other Pueblo Indians, the Cochiti built their homes long ago near the Rio Grande River. Our climate is dry, but the river gives us water all year round for raising our corn and wheat. The river makes the alfalfa we plant grow green and lush, so the cattle in our pastures are fat and healthy.

There are many different pueblos along the Rio Grande River, but the Indians who live in them do not all belong to the same tribe. Since their ancestors came from different places, they speak different languages. But their traditions and way of life are very similar.

In many ways, pueblo life is the same today as it was in the old days. People still live in adobe *(a-DOH-bee)* houses. Just as our ancestors did, the Cochiti people make adobe bricks by mixing the clay found near our village with straw from the fields and water from the river. When the bricks dry, they are very strong and we use them to build our homes. These houses, made of earth, keep us warm in the winter and cool in the summer.

2

Home and family have always been important to the Pueblo Indians. I am lucky to have a big, happy family. My grandparents, my uncle and two aunts, my little cousin, and I all live together in one house. But there is sadness, too. When I was three years old, my mother died, and I have lived with my grandparents ever since.

People in our pueblo still plant and harvest crops of corn, beans, and squash. As they did long ago, they make beautiful pottery and drums. The people in our pueblo sing the same songs and perform the same dances as our ancestors did. They celebrate some of the same religious holidays and festivals, too.

But some things are different. Today many people leave the pueblo each day to work in Santa Fe or Albuquerque. It is hard to survive in the modern world without the income from a job.

In the past, the only way to get an education was to go to a boarding school in the city. These students lived at the school and came home on weekends or holidays. Now there are schools at each pueblo, so children can learn close to their homes.

Every morning, I ride the bus across the Rio Grande River and up a long hill to my school. One of my favorite classes is music, where I am learning to play the saxophone. My best song is "Twinkle, Twinkle, Little Star."

Each day I take a class in Keres. We learn to pronounce the words and read stories in our own language. These tales help us to imagine Cochiti life as it was in the past.

We went on a field trip to Old Mesa and climbed among the ruins where our tribal ancestors once lived. All the doorways we found there were very small. We had to stoop down to get inside. Long ago, the doorways were made that way to keep the heat in and the cold out. My teacher says that our ancestors were also much shorter than we are today—only about four feet high. I am just ten and I am taller than that already!

Although we live in the modern world, we like to stay close to nature, to the old ways and traditions. We learn about these traditions from our parents and grandparents.

April and her cousin have fun together on the slide in their front yard.

April likes to play golf with her grandfather after school. The tribe owns and operates the public course near Cochiti Lake, where they play.

3

Late in the afternoon, April goes next door to shoot some baskets with a friend. They like to play a game called Horse.

4

Baking the Bread

My grandmother shows me how to make bread in the traditional way. In the Keres language, the bread is called ba'a *(BAH)*.

My grandmother makes ba'a on special occasions when we have many guests, such as our feast days and dances. She mixes flour, lard, yeast, and water. She doesn't use a recipe. She puts it together the way her mother taught her. She knows how the dough should look and how it should feel as she works with it. Now she teaches me.

When my grandmother makes bread, she bakes many, many loaves. We never know exactly how many loaves of bread there will be when she is finished. She tells us of an old Indian saying: "If you count the bread, you'll run out." So we never count. We never worry if we'll have enough. Somehow there is always ba'a for everyone.

April and her cousin help their grandmother shape the bread dough into round loaves.

April's grandmother uses a long wooden paddle to slide the loaves of bread dough into the hot oven. The doors of the horno always face the east. Because the wind blows from the west, this helps to keep sand from blowing into the open door of the oven.

After mixing the dough, we set it in a warm place so the yeast can make it rise. It grows and grows until it is double in size. Then we knead the dough and shape it into loaves to bake in the ovens outside. These outdoor ovens are shaped like a beehive and are called by the Spanish name horno *(HOR-noh)*. In Keres, the oven is called korsch-t-co *(KORSCH-tee-koh)*.

Nearly every pueblo home has at least one horno in the yard. The Cochiti build the hornos from layers of stones. Then they seal the stones with a smooth covering of adobe mud to hold the heat inside.

My grandparents make a big fire in the oven with branches of cedar. After the fire has burned for about an hour, they sweep the coals out with a wet broom. They wipe the ashes from the floor of the oven with a damp cloth. The fire is gone, but the heat stays trapped in the stone walls. Now the oven is the right temperature for baking.

My grandmother covers the oven floor with the loaves of bread dough and watches as they bake. She knows by the toasty brown color of the crust and the mouth-watering smell when the bread is finished.

My grandmother takes the loaves from the oven with a long wooden paddle. We have plenty of ba'a for our family and more to share with others.

We eat the bread with red chili and posole *(pah-SOH-lay)*, two of our traditional pueblo foods. The red chili is made by cooking beef with ground red chili peppers. It is very spicy and it makes my mouth burn! Posole is a soup made with roasted white corn and meat.

To make posole, my grandmother sets some ears of corn out to dry in the sun. Then she roasts them over hot coals until they are toasted a light brown. She scrapes the kernels off the cobs and adds them to a broth made with beef or pork. When the roasted corn kernels cook in the broth, they pop open, like popcorn. Posole is delicious!

April and her family enjoy the fresh baked ba'a with their lunch of red chili and posole.

Making the Pottery

The shadows are already long when April and her grandfather return to their pueblo with a load of clay. In the background are the Sandia Mountains.

My grandmother and grandfather make pottery in the traditional pueblo way. They do the work together. They do everything by hand. My grandmother learned to make pottery from her mother. Then she taught her daughters. Now she teaches me.

Making fine pottery has always been important to the pueblo people. The clay pots made by our ancestors were used for cooking, serving, and storing food. Sometimes pots were traded to other tribes. Today, there is at least one person in every Cochiti household who knows how to make pottery. Often pueblo families earn their living by selling the beautiful pots and figures that they make from the clay.

Each of the pueblos has its own place to get clay. The potters dig it from the ground. The clay comes in many natural colors. There are reds and browns and grays. There is even a pure white clay. Pueblo people make an offering of blue corn to thank the earth for providing the clay. Some families have gone to the same place to get the clay for generations.

My grandfather takes me with him when he goes for the clay. He drives to a faraway mesa where he can dig it from the ground. This is hard work!

Sometimes he has to crawl through a long tunnel of earth to find the clay. My grandfather uses a pick and a shovel to dig it out. We carry it back to our truck in buckets.

April helps her grandfather carry the clay back to the truck. Going for the clay is hard work, but April enjoys the time outdoors. Her grandfather tells her about the plants and animals they see on the way. Once they found the tracks of a mountain lion!

When it comes from the ground, the clay is hard and dry.

April's grandfather kneads the fine sand into the clay indoors, where the wind will not blow it away.

The clay is hard, like a rock. My grandfather soaks it in water until it becomes soft enough to work with his hands. He collects white sand from another place in the pueblo. He sifts the sand to remove the large rocks, sticks, and pebbles. Then he works the fine sand into the red clay to give it texture and make it stronger.

I like to watch my grandfather as he works. He kneads the clay together with the sand in the same way that my grandmother and I knead the dough for our bread. He works the clay with his hands until it feels just right.

When the clay is ready, my grandmother takes it and shows me how to begin. First we make a flat piece called a slab, and then we curve it to form a cylinder. This shape becomes the body of the clay figure my grandmother teaches me to make. It is the figure of a Pueblo Storyteller.

Since the early days of pueblo life, our people have learned about the past by listening to storytellers. Until now, we have never had a written language, so many of our stories cannot be found in books. This is why the storyteller is such an important person in our culture. This is also why so many potters in the Cochiti Pueblo make clay figures of the storyteller.

When my grandmother makes a Storyteller, she always thinks about her own grandfather. When she was a young girl, she enjoyed many happy hours in his company. In those days, they didn't have a television or a gas heater. She would sit on her grandfather's lap near a little fireplace in the corner of the room and listen to him tell stories about his life.

Working on the clay figure, my grandmother creates a face that looks like her grandfather's. She gives him the traditional hairstyle of a pueblo man from the old days. She models the clay to show his long hair pulled back in a loop behind his head with a colorful band to hold it in place.

My grandmother makes arms and legs from smaller cylinders. She attaches these to the body with bits of moistened clay. Then she models boots or moccasins from the clay.

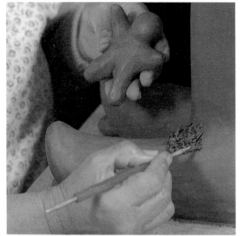

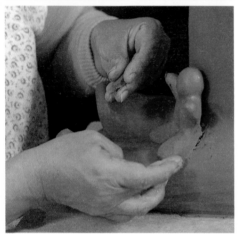

April's grandmother makes the figure of a little child. Then she attaches the child to the body of the Storyteller with bits of moistened clay.

A Storyteller is left to dry in the corner of the kitchen. On the shelf above the clay figure, you can see a ladle made from a gourd.

She always makes his face look very kind. He sits with his mouth open, as if he were singing a song or telling a story. His eyes are closed as he thinks in the backward way, remembering the past.

Each potter who makes a Storyteller figure works in a different style. Some Storytellers are large and some are small. Many potters create the figure of a woman, remembering a favorite aunt or grandmother. Others, like my grandmother, design a figure that reminds them of their grandfather.

When the Storyteller is complete, my grandmother makes many tiny figures out of the clay. These are shaped like little pueblo children and she attaches them, one by one, to the Storyteller figure. She crowds them all onto his lap, so they can listen carefully to his tales, just as she did so long ago.

My grandmother adds as many children as she can fit. She tells me that on every Storyteller she makes, there is one child who looks just like me! This makes me feel very special.

After all the modeling is finished, the pottery is left to dry. This takes many days.

When the Storyteller has been painted, it is ready for the firing. All the colors on the figure are natural and were made by hand from clay and plants found on the Cochiti lands. In the painting, April's grandmother has given each little child a different expression. Some are happy and some are sad, some are sleepy and some are mad. Like real children, they express many moods. But they are all gathered together on the Storyteller's lap to hear his tales. They all share the same history.

April's grandfather shows her how to sand a Storyteller. Sanding makes the surface smooth enough to paint.

April carefully sands a small turtle she made. Many pueblo children make little turtles out of clay when they are first beginning to learn about pottery. The turtle is an important creature in pueblo legends and children often find them outdoors near their homes.

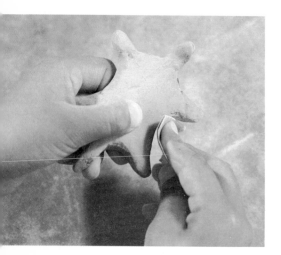

When the pottery is hard and dry, it is my grandfather's turn to work on it. He rubs the surfaces of the pottery with sandpaper until they are smooth enough to paint. My grandfather tells me he likes to be in a happy, patient mood when he is sanding the pottery. The work must be done carefully. It cannot be rushed.

Sometimes the pottery will break or crack before it is finished. Instead of throwing the ruined pottery away in the garbage, the pueblo potters give the clay back to the earth where it came from. My grandfather often takes a broken pot down to the river and throws it in the water. Sometimes he will take the broken pieces back up into the hills near the pueblo.

After the pieces are sanded, my grandmother covers them with a thin layer of white clay that has been mixed with water, called slip *(SLIP)*. When the slip dries, it gives the pottery a clean, white surface that can be polished and painted.

To get a shiny surface, my grandmother polishes her pots with special stones. These polishing stones are very important to the pueblo potters. Each one gives a different patina or shine. Polishing stones are treasured, and the good ones are passed down from one generation to the next.

My grandmother likes to paint her pottery in a very quiet place. She needs to concentrate so that the lines she draws will be straight and the shapes that she makes will be beautiful.

For the red color, my grandmother uses a clay that is mixed with water. For the black, she uses guaco (*GWA-koh*), an inky liquid made by boiling down a wild plant that grows in the fields near our house. It is called Rocky Mountain beeweed. This same plant is something we pick in the spring and eat as one of our vegetables.

After my grandmother finishes painting the pottery, it is time for the firing. This is the final step. Firing the pottery makes the clay very strong so it will last for a long time.

(Left) April's grandmother rubs the bottom of a pot with a polishing stone that came to her from her mother. On her work table are bowls of red clay mixed with water and guaco.

(Right) Working carefully, April's grandmother begins to paint a colorful design on a pot covered with a layer of white slip. She holds it with a soft cloth to keep her fingerprints from getting on the pot.

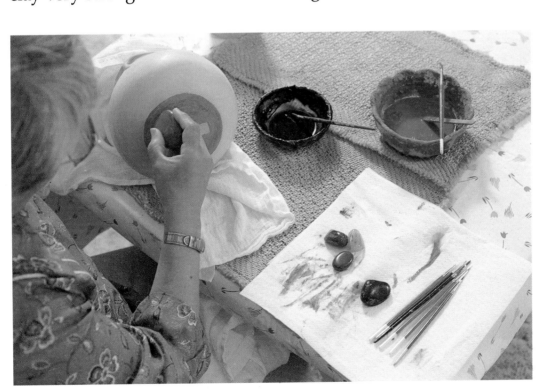

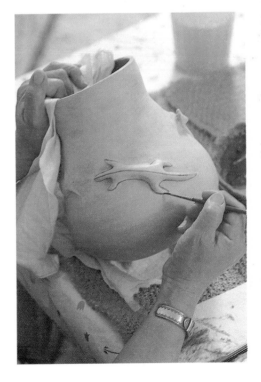

15

The flat, dry cow pies are placed in a single layer all around the pottery.

My grandparents work together to build a kiln *(KILN)* outside in the yard. They go out to the pasture and collect many pieces of dried cow manure. We call these "cow pies" because they are so flat and round. My grandparents lay some wood under a metal grate and put the pottery on top of it. They arrange the cow pies in a single layer on the top and sides of the pottery.

The cow pies are mostly made of grass, and they burn easily. They make the fire all around the pottery burn evenly at a very high temperature. We burn cow pies instead of wood because they do not contain pitch or sap that could stain the beautifully painted surfaces of the pottery.

After the fire is lit, we can only watch and wait. When the fire burns out and the pottery cools, my grandmother rakes the ashes away. We carefully remove the pottery and clean off any small bits of grit or ash. "Now the work is finished," my grandfather tells me proudly. "It is perfect and beautiful, made by our own hands from the earth's elements of fire, water, and clay."

Sticks of cedar wood on the sides catch fire as the kiln begins to burn. The fire spreads to the cow pies underneath.

Making the Cochiti Drum

Sometimes my grandmother likes to make a clay figure that looks like a man playing the Cochiti drum. The Cochiti people are famous for the drums they make. My own uncle is a drum maker.

My uncle makes drums of every size. He makes the tiny ones for my grandmother's clay figures. He also makes small drums for children, large drums for trading, and special ceremonial drums for our pueblo dances.

My uncle begins with the trunk of a large aspen or cottonwood tree. He saws it into drum-size lengths. Then he scrapes the bark off with a drawknife. Using hot coals, he carefully burns a hole down the middle of the log to make it hollow. Then he uses a handmade chisel to cut away more wood. When this is done, he has completed the drum frame.

To make the head of the drum, my uncle uses a large piece of cowhide. The hide has been soaked in water so it is soft and easy to bend. He cuts two round pieces that fit over the top and bottom of the drum frame. Then, with a long, thin cord cut from the hide, he sews them together in a zigzag pattern.

My uncle tightens the cords, one by one, until the drumheads are firm. As the wet hide dries, the drumheads get tighter and tighter.

Every drum my uncle makes has its own special sound, its own voice. Because the drums are made by hand, each one makes a different sound. When they are finished, my uncle plays them. Some are loud and some are soft. Some are high and some are low. Some rumble like thunder and others rat-tat-tat like dry leaves in the wind.

The clay drummer holds a small Cochiti drum and a beater made from an alder stick and deer hide. The tiny drum makes a very tiny sound.

With a handmade chisel, April's uncle cuts away the wood in the center of a log to make a drum frame. He says that homemade tools work better and last longer than the tools he can buy at the store.

April's uncle uses a drawknife to remove the bark from an alder log. He reaches out, cuts into the bark, and then pulls the knife back toward his body.

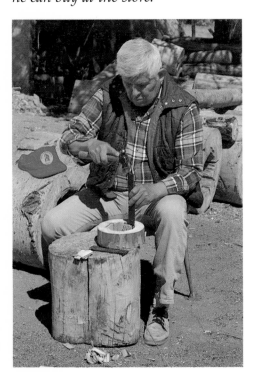

Using a tool made from the fork in a tree branch, April's uncle draws a ring on the hide large enough for the head of a small, child's drum.

Painting the drum is the very last step. April's uncle shows her how the painted designs make each drum special. On this drum, the black shapes represent the sky and the white shapes are clouds.

When we play the drums in a pueblo ceremony, the voices of the drums mix with the voices of the singers to make music for the dancers.

My uncle learned to make drums by watching his foster father work. He is proud to know the way to make an instrument with a beautiful, strong voice. He likes to work with his hands and he shares what he knows with me.

The Buffalo Dance

In the pueblos along the Rio Grande, children learn to dance almost as soon as they learn to walk. We all have drums in our homes that we play. Our parents and grandparents sing to us and show us the way to move.

Dances are performed at our Pueblo Feast Day and for special ceremonies. Everyone takes part. On these occasions, we gather in the plaza. This large open space is the center of pueblo life.

As the singers begin to chant their songs in our ancient Indian language, the drums begin to sound. The singer is the storyteller and the voice of the drum is his music.

The singer plays a special dance drum, painted with the images of an Indian and a buffalo head. The colors on the sides stand for the four directions of the earth: white is for north, red is for south, blue is for east, and yellow is for west.

April joins two Tewa boys from San Juan Pueblo for the Buffalo Dance. They take small steps as they move to the drumbeats. The boys, dressed in buffalo headdresses, carry a lightning bolt in one hand and a gourd rattle in the other. They wear embroidered kilts.

For this dance, April wears a special necklace made of a seashell decorated with tiny turquoise stones. She holds a bunch of bright parrot feathers. The Pueblo Indians lived in a desert climate far from any ocean, so they traded for these things with tribes from Mexico and Central America.

The dancers move in patterns passed down from one generation to the next. The dances we do today are very much like the dances our ancestors performed hundreds of years ago.

The Buffalo Dance is one of these. It began a long time ago, when there were large herds of buffalo on the western Plains. Our ancestors crossed the mountains to the north to hunt the buffalo. They often traded the hides to other Indians on the Plains. They always carried the meat back to the pueblo to help their people survive the long winter months.

Sometimes we dance to have a successful hunt or to bring rains to our dry lands. Sometimes we dance to have a fruitful harvest or to cure the sick. And sometimes we dance just for fun!

(Left) Eagle feathers decorate the back of the Buffalo dancer's headdress.

(Right) The dancer's moccasins have a fringe of squirrel fur. The embroidered kilts and crocheted leggings are made by hand.

Pueblo Storyteller

For me there is a special time at the end of every day. After the work is finished and I am ready to go to bed, my grandmother and grandfather tell me stories from the past. Sometimes they tell about the legends of the pueblo people. Other times they tell about things that happened in their own lives.

My grandmother likes to tell about when she was a girl. She lived in a Tewa *(TAY-wah)* pueblo to the north called San Juan. She remembers autumn, a time when her whole family worked together to harvest and husk the corn crop. The corn came in many colors—red and orange, yellow and white, blue and purple, and even the deepest black.

Her family would sit in the shade of a ramada *(rah-MAH-dah)* built of cedar branches. Sheltered from the hot sun, the workers would remove the husks from a mountain of colorful corn. All the time they were working, they would laugh at jokes, sing songs, and share stories.

My grandmother tells me there were always lots of children around—her brothers and sisters, their cousins and friends—and they always had fun. My grandfather tells how the boys would use their slingshots to hurl stones at the crows who came too close to the corncobs that were drying in the sun.

As I listen to their stories, I can almost hear the sound of laughter as the children play at their games. I can smell the bread baking as the women prepare to feed their families. I can see the mounds of corn, colored like the rainbow, drying in the sun.

When I was very young, my grandparents told me a legend about how our ancestors found the place where we are living today, our pueblo along the Rio Grande River. They call it "How the People Came to Earth," and it is still one of my favorite tales.

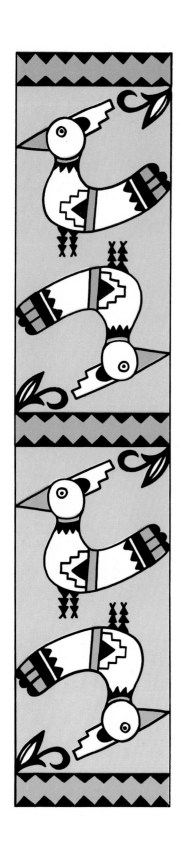

How the People Came to Earth
A PUEBLO LEGEND

Long, long ago, our people wandered from place to place across the universe. Their leader was Long Sash, the star that we call Orion. He was the great warrior of the skies. Long Sash told his people that he had heard of a land far away, a place where they could make a home.

Because the people were weary of wandering, they decided to follow Long Sash on the dangerous journey across the sky to search for a new home. They traveled on the Endless Trail, the river of countless stars that we call the Milky Way.

The way was hard for our people. Long Sash taught them to hunt for food, and to make clothing from the skins of animals and the feathers of birds. Even so, they were often hungry and cold, and many died along the way. Long Sash led them farther than any people had ever gone before.

After a time, the people came to a vast darkness, and they were afraid. But Long Sash, the great warrior, believed they were heading the right way, and led them on. Suddenly, they heard the faint sound of scratching. Then, as they watched, a tiny speck of light appeared in the distance. As they got nearer, the light grew larger and larger. Then they saw that it was a small hole leading to another world.

When they looked through the opening, they saw a little mole digging away in the earth. Long Sash thanked the mole for helping them to find their way out of the darkness. But the mole only replied, "Come in to our world. And when you see the sign of my footprints again, you will know you have found your true home." The people saw a cord hanging down from the hole and they all climbed up and went through into the new world.

Once through the opening, Long Sash saw Old Spider Woman busily weaving her web. He asked permission to pass through her house. Old Spider Woman replied, "You may come through my house. But when you next see the sign of my spiderweb, you will have found your true home."

The people did not understand what Old Spider Woman meant, but they thanked her and continued on their journey.

Long Sash and his followers traveled to many places on the earth. They found lands of ice and snow, lands where the sun burned and the air was dry, and beautiful lands with tall trees and plenty of game for hunting. In all of these places, they searched for signs of the mole and Old Spider Woman, but found nothing.

Some of the people stayed behind in the lands they discovered, but Long Sash and most of the tribe kept going. They kept searching for their true home.

Finally they came to a new land where the seasons were wet and dry, hot and cold, with good soil and bad. They found, here and there, small tracks that looked like a mole's. They followed the tracks and found a strange-looking creature, with ugly, wrinkled skin. The slow-moving animal carried a rounded shell on its back.

Long Sash was very happy when he saw the creature. "Look!" he said. "He carries his home with him, as we have done these many years. He travels slowly, just like us. On his shell are the markings of the spiderweb and his tracks look just like the mole's."

When our people saw the turtle, they knew they had found the homeland they had traveled the universe to discover. And we still live on those same lands today.

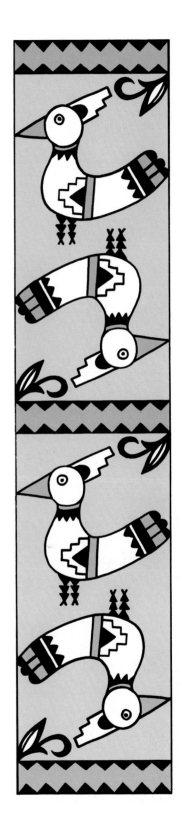

April's grandmother shows the children a pot made by her mother. The design on the side shows a serpent called Awanyu (a-WAN-yoo) by the Pueblo Indians. She tells them how the serpent, a creature who lives in water, was sacred to their ancestors as they struggled to survive in a dry land.

My grandparents are storytellers who have brought the past alive for me through their memories, through their language, through their art, and even through the food we eat. I am thankful that they have given me this rich history. From them I have learned to bake bread in an ancient way, to work with the earth's gift of clay, and to dance to the music of the Cochiti drums.

I am a pueblo child and I love to listen to my grandparents tell stories. From their example, I learn to take what I need from the earth to live, but also how to leave something behind for future generations. Every day I am learning to live in harmony with the world. And every day, I am collecting memories of my life to share one day with my own children and grandchildren.

GLOSSARY

Adobe: *(a-DOH-bee)* Sun-dried brick made from clay and straw. The Pueblo Indians use adobe to build their homes.

Alfalfa: A plant with small leaves and cloverlike flowers grown as a crop for cattle and horses to eat.

Awanyu: *(a-WAN-yoo)* The pueblo word for serpent.

Ba'a: *(BAH)* A Keres word for the bread made in the pueblo style and baked in an outdoor oven.

Chili: The dried pod of the red pepper used in pueblo cooking as a hot, spicy seasoning.

Cochiti: *(KOH-chi-tee)* A Pueblo Indian tribe of the Keres language group living along the Rio Grande River in New Mexico.

Cow pies: A slang term for round, dried pieces of cow manure.

Drawknife: A sharp tool with two handles used to remove the bark from a tree trunk.

Foster father: A person who acts as a father to a child but who has no blood relationship with that child.

Gourd: The dried, hollowed-out shell of the fruit of a plant belonging to the squash, melon, or pumpkin families. The pueblo people used gourds for drinking cups and dippers.

Guaco: *(GWA-koh)* The black, sticky substance made by boiling down Rocky Mountain beeweed, a wild plant. The pueblo potters use guaco as a black paint for their pottery.

Horno: *(HOR-noh)* A Spanish word for the beehive-shaped outdoor ovens found in the Rio Grande pueblos. The pueblo people bake a bread called ba'a in the hornos.

Keres: *(CARE-ees)* The ancient Indian language spoken by the pueblo people of Cochiti, Acoma, San Felipe, Santa Ana, Santo Domingo, Zia, and Laguna.

Kiln: *(KILN)* An oven or furnace that is used to bake pottery at a high temperature. The pueblo potters build a new kiln each time they fire their pottery.

Kilt: A knee-length skirt, usually of cotton, worn for dances and ceremonial occasions by pueblo men and boys.

Korsch-t-co: *(KORSCH-tee-koh)* The Keres word for the beehive-shaped ovens used by the pueblo people to bake bread.

KU-tsi-ya-t'si: *(KOO-tsee-yahtz)* A Keres word that means "Lady Antelope."

Leggings: Coverings for the legs, usually crocheted, worn by pueblo men and boys for dances and ceremonial occasions.

Manta: *(MON-tah)* A short dress, usually made of black cotton, that covers one shoulder and is pinned on the side. The manta is worn over a cotton print dress by pueblo women and girls for dances and ceremonial occasions.

Mesa: *(MAY-sah)* A high flat mountain with steep sides.

Posole: *(pah-SOH-lay)* A traditional pueblo dish made with roasted white corn and a meat broth.

Pueblo: *(PWEB-loh)* A Spanish word for village or town.

Ramada: *(rah-MAH-dah)* A shelter from the sun made of four upright posts and a roof of branches. All four sides are open to the air. The Pueblo Indians worked under the ramada when doing outside jobs like husking corn.

Rio Grande River: Rio Grande means "Big River" in Spanish. It is 1,885 miles long and flows through Colorado, New Mexico, and Texas.

Rocky Mountain beeweed: A wild plant used both as a vegetable in the spring and boiled down to make guaco for painting pottery later in the year.

Slip: *(SLIP)* A white clay mixed with water used to coat pottery to give it a clean, light surface that can be painted.

Tewa: *(TAY-wah)* An ancient Indian language spoken by the pueblo people in San Juan, Tesuque, Santa Clara, San Ildefonso, Pojoaque, and Nambe.

INDEX

Numbers in *italics* refer to pages with photos.

adobe bricks, 2, *2*

ba'a (bread) 5, *5*, 7
bread baking, 5–7, 26
buffalo, 22
Buffalo Dance, *20*, 22

clay, 2, 8–10, 16, 26
   red, 15
   returning to earth, 14
   working, 10
Cochiti, 1, 2
Cochiti drum, 17, 26
corn, 3, 7, 23
cow pies, 16, *16*

dancing, 3, 20, 22, 26
drawknife, *18*
drums, 17–20
   for dancing, *20*
   designs on, *19, 20*
   making, 17–18

guaco, 15

horno (oven), *6*, 6–7
"How the People Came to Earth," 23–25

jewelry, *1, 21*

Keres, 1, 3
kiln, 16

manta, *1*

Old Mesa, 3

polishing stones, 15, *15*
posole, 7
pottery making, 8–16
   firing, 15–16
   modeling, 10–12
   painting, 15
   polishing, 15
   sanding, 14

ramada, 23
red chili, 7
Rio Grande, 2, *2*, 20, 23
Rocky Mountain beeweed, 15

school, 3
slip, 14, *15*
storytellers, 10, 11, 20, 23, 26

turtle, 14, 25